BUTTERFLIES & MOTHS

A PORTRAIT OF THE ANIMAL WORLD

Paul Sterry

NEW LINE BOOKS

Fax: (888) 719-7723
e-mail: info@newlinebooks.com

Printed and bound in Korea

ISBN 1-59764-114-6

Visit us on the web!
www.newlinebooks.com

PHOTO CREDITS

Photographer/Page Number

Aquila Photographics
J. P. Black 45 (bottom)
J. Corton 33 (bottom)
Sawford/Castle 67 (bottom)
M. Gilroy 5, 11 (top), 15 (bottom), 36 (bottom), 51, 53 (top)
N. W. Harwood 21, 63, 74, 79
Adrian Hoskins 45 (top), 46 (top)
Mike Lane 12 (top)
T. Leach 47 (top), 49 (bottom)
R. T. Mills 68 (bottom)

Harry N. Darrow 14 (bottom), 46 (bottom), 56-57, 77 (top)

Dembinsky Photo Associates
Russ Gutshall 18
Skip Moody 59, 72-73
Rod Planck 8-9, 69, 70

Stephen Kirkpatrick 6

Joe McDonald 12 (bottom), 60

Nature Photographers Ltd.
Andrew Cleave 17

Edward S. Ross 14 (top), 20 (bottom), 23, 28 (bottom), 33 (top), 36 (top),
43 (top), 47 (bottom), 49 (middle), 50 (top), 52, 71 (bottom)

Gail Shumway 3, 11 (bottom), 13, 15 (top), 22, 26, 27, 28 (top), 31, 32,
34 (top), 34 (bottom), 35 (top), 35 (bottom), 37, 38, 44, 48, 53 (bottom), 54 (top), 54 (bottom),
55, 57 (top), 57 (bottom), 58, 64 (top), 66, 75, 76 (bottom), 77 (bottom)

Tom Stack & Associates
John Gerlach 24-25, 40-41
Kerry Givens 65
Don & Esther Phillips 16, 20 (top), 39
Milton Rand 7, 71 (top), 76 (top)
John Shaw 4, 42, 43 (bottom)
Larry Tackett 61 (top), 64 (bottom)
Denise Tackett 29

The Wildlife Collection
Kenneth Deitcher 10
Tim Laman 19, 61 (bottom), 67 (top)
Clay Myers 68 (top)
Bob Parks 62, 78
Jack Swenson 30, 49 (top)

INTRODUCTION

The patterns seen on the underwings of this Malaysian lacewing (Cethosia hypsea) are extremely striking. It is often the case that forest species have bright colours or strong markings, which presumably facilitate recognition by others of the same species.

Imagine a warm summer morning in an ancient oak woodland in southern England. Shafts of sunlight begin to cut through the tree canopy and cast bright highlights on the leaves carpeting the woodland floor. Suddenly a shadow passes over the leaves as a purple emperor (Apatura iris) takes its first flight of the day. One of the largest of European butterflies, it glides gracefully toward the ground where it visits a muddy puddle to drink.

With wings closed, the beautifully marked orange-brown underwings are revealed. Occasionally, however, the purple emperor nervously flicks open its wings revealing truly splen-

did upperwings. At certain angles these look brown and white, but when the light is right, a magnificent metallic-purple sheen is seen, and the contrast between the two surfaces will astonish any onlooker.

The butterfly drinks for several minutes and is joined by a range of other insects. Soon, its thirst quenched, it flies powerfully upward to spend the rest of the day disputing territories and searching for mates amongst the crowns of the tallest oak trees.

The following text explains the internal functions and structure of butterflies and moths, referred to collectively as Lepidoptera—which can be literally translated as 'scale-wing', a reference to the coating of scales found on the wings of most species. The range of species found throughout the world is explored as are their day-to-day lives and their fascinating life cycles. With nearly 150,000 species of Lepidoptera known in the world, and many yet to be discovered, there is certainly no shortage of subject matter for study.

The emergence of a butterfly, such as this monarch (Danaus plexippus), from a pupa is one of the true miracles of nature. The metamorphosis may take a matter of only a few minutes, but it is preceded by weeks of complex changes in the internal structure of the insect.

Using its long proboscis, this monarch (Danaus plexippus) is probing a flower for nectar. When not feeding, butterflies can coil up this apparatus; it then becomes partly hidden beneath the head.

BUTTERFLIES AND MOTHS AS INSECTS

Butterflies and moths belong to a group of invertebrate animals called insects, themselves members of a larger systematic grouping called the Arthropods. Insects are extremely varied both in terms of size and appearance but all the members of this group share certain characteristics. Insects have an external skeleton made of a hardened proteinlike material called chitin and, more fundamentally, all adult insect bodies are divided into three distinct sections: the head, the thorax, and the abdomen.

The head bears important sensory organs including the eyes and antennae as well as the mouthparts; the thorax carries three pairs of legs and the wings, of which there are two pairs visible in almost all cases; the abdomen, which is segmented, contains the reproductive, excretory, and digestive systems. Like all insects, butterflies and moths have life cycles

The wings of a butterfly are covered with layers of tiny scales, arranged like roofing tiles. The scales are pigmented and produce the colour we so admire, such as in this western tiger swallowtail (Pterourus rutulus).

Resting on tree bark, this tulip tree beauty (Epimecis bortaria) is amazingly well camouflaged. Moths with such cryptic patterning are usually adept at positioning themselves for best effect.

Following page:
At rest, the hindwings of the io moth are hidden by the forewings. When alarmed, however, these are spread to reveal startling eyespots, which have the effect of temporarily putting off would-be predators.

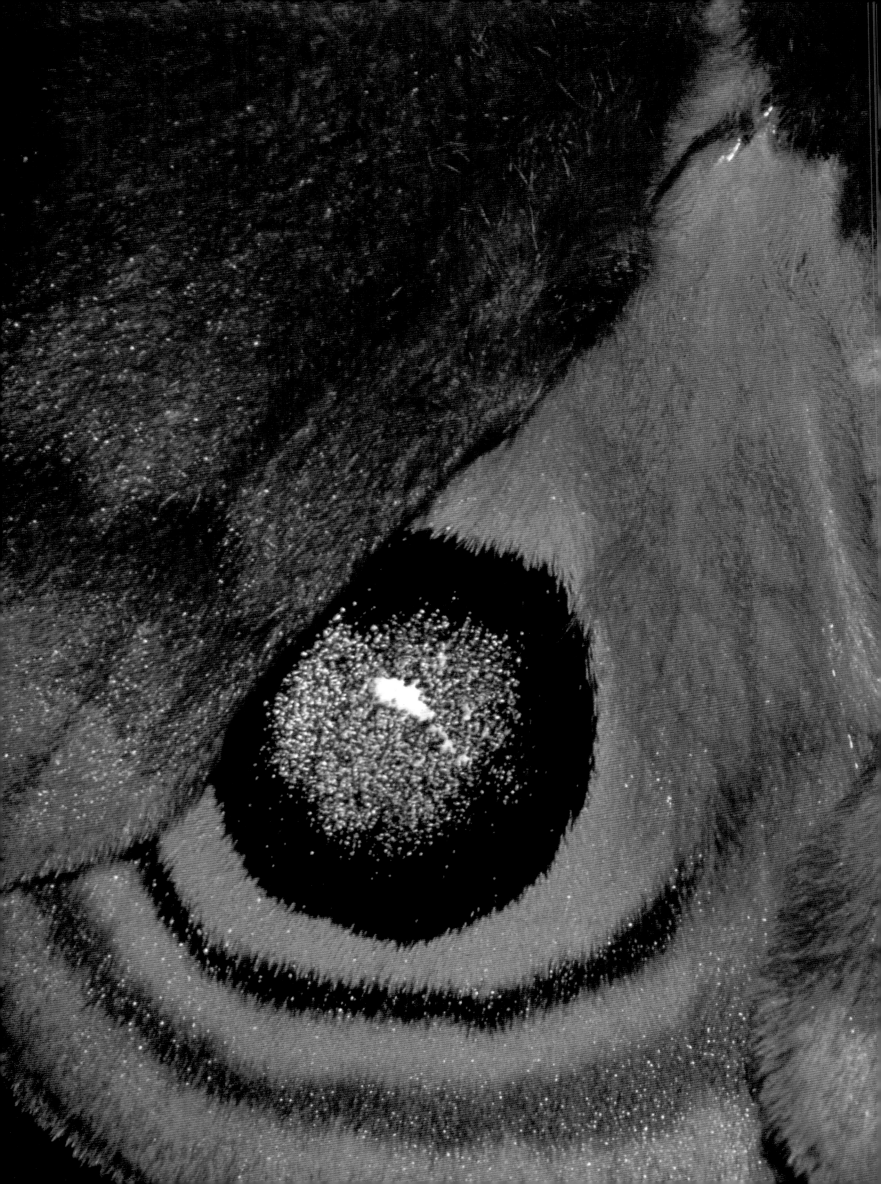

that involve several very different stages. In the case of Lepidoptera, these comprise the egg, the caterpillar or larva, the chrysalis or pupa, and the adult.

Although butterflies and moths are closely related and are both termed Lepidoptera, there are subtle differences between the two. The way that most of us tell at a glance whether we are looking at a butterfly or at a moth is usually by whether it is flying during the day or at night. Butterflies are day-flying insects and, by and large, are only active when the sun is shining. Moths, on the other hand, are largely nocturnal, venturing out to feed only after dark. There are, as one might expect, exceptions to these rules, especially in the moth world, in which there are plenty of examples of day-flying species. The shape of the antennae (discussed below) can also be a useful means of distinguishing between butterflies and moths, as can the way that the wings are held at rest: butterflies usually rest with wings folded over their backs while moths rest with the wings out flat.

The Head

Possessing two antennae, two large eyes, and a proboscis, the head of a butterfly or moth is vital to its survival. With it the insect gets all the information it needs about the world around it, and, in many species, it is utilised to imbibe vital nutrients.

The eyes of adult insects, including butterflies and moths, are called compound eyes and are very different in structure from, for example, conventional mammalian eyes. Instead of having a single lens focusing light onto a light-receptive layer at the back of the eye, butterfly eyes are made up of thousands of elongated cells called ommatidia, each of which contains a tiny lens and a receptor. Each ommatidium forms an image of its own and thousands of these are combined to create an overall pattern. Because butterfly eyes are hemispherical, a wide angle of vision is encompassed. However, the compound image is not so well formed as the image humans see with their eyes. Insects are very good at detecting movement but not very capable of picking out fine details. They are, however, perfectly able to carry on their lives, often using specific colours or ultraviolet petal markers to locate flowers for feeding.

The flexibility of a butterfly's proboscis can be seen clearly in this photograph. This great orange tip (Hebomoia glaucippe) probes deep into the nectaries of this flower in search of food.

The males of luna moths (Actius luna), together with many of their relatives, have large, feathery antennae. The increased surface area this provides enables them to detect with greater efficiency the scent given off by female moths.

Beautiful salmon-pink patches and a rich marbling of brown, buff, and black adorn the underwings of this American painted lady (Vanessa virginiensis). Two eyespots on the underside of the hindwing distinguish this species from a similar painted lady (Vanessa cardui), which has four or five.

The antennae of butterflies and moths are usually very conspicuous when the insect is active, although they may be partly hidden when at rest. They are important sensory organs in everyday life, aiding with balance in flight and with the detection of smells. In most species the antennae are long and straight. Butterfly antennae are normally clubbed at the tip while those of most moths are slender and tapering. An exception can be found in the feathery antennae of certain male moths.

Antennae are used to locate flowers, which are a rich source of nectar for butterflies and moths. Many plants give off a fragrance that lures insects to feed from them; in return,

insects unwittingly carry pollen from one flower to another. Antennae are also used to find a mate. In many (and probably all) species, the female exudes a special chemical called a pheromone which helps the male to locate her. This is clearly more important in some species than in others. Male emperor moths *(Pavonia pavonia)*, for example, have antennae that are large and feathery, thus increasing their surface area in order to better detect a mate. So acute is their sense of smell that males can detect a female downwind at a range of up to a kilometre or so, and often before she has fully emerged from her cocoon.

Although the adults of some butterfly and moth species do not feed per se, most have strong appetites. They do not possess biting or chewing mouthparts like other insects such as beetles, or indeed as they do in their own larval stage, and instead have a proboscis which is used to feed on liquid food sources. This comprises a long, slender tube that is held coiled and at least partly hidden when the insect is not feeding. It can be unraveled at will and inserted into the nectar-bearing parts of flowers, which are themselves often adapted to suit the mouthparts of a particular species.

Skippers are active little butterflies which share certain affinities with moths. They occur wherever their larval foodplants—grasses— flourish; this individual (Polites sabuleta) was photographed in California.

Although strikingly marked and extremely colourful, this species is in fact a moth and not a butterfly. The best clue to this lies in the shape of the antennae, which are slightly feathery and not uniform along their length.

Flowery meadows full of thistles are home to the American painted lady (Vanessa virginiensis), widespread throughout North America wherever suitable habitats occur. This attractive butterfly is an active flier.

This appealing blue pansy butterfly (Junonia orithya) rests and feeds on a colourful flower. This species can be reared in captivity and will thrive if its liking for tropical conditions be borne in mind.

Most butterflies and many moths feed while resting on the flower in question. Some moths, particularly many of the large hawkmoths and a few tropical butterflies, actually feed on the wing. Species such as the convolvulus hawkmoth *(Agrius convolvuli)* unravel a proboscis several inches long and will feed on the flowers of tobacco plants. Although smaller, the hummingbird hawkmoth *(Macroglossum stellatarum)* can often be seen feeding during the daytime in a similar manner on the flowers of red valerian.

The Thorax and Abdomen

The thorax can be said to be the powerhouse of a butterfly or moth's body. It is the part of the body to which the wings and legs are attached and contains important muscle blocks used in movement. Because they have an external skeleton, the muscles of insects have to be located internally, and those of butterflies and moths are no exception.

In adult insects there are three pairs of legs.

Because they have a rigid external skeleton, the legs are jointed in several places along their length, the angle of each joint slightly different from the one next to it. This allows for a surprising degree of mobility. Each leg is divided into four sections; from the point of attachment of the leg to the body these are the coxa, femur, tibia, and tarsus. The tarsus carries structures which provide good gripping capability, and also bear sensory hairs that in effect 'taste' whatever the butterfly or moth is resting upon.

The most obvious feature of the abdomen is that it is segmented. The chitin that forms each segment is not as hard as other parts of the butterfly body, and is linked together by flexible, membranelike chitin. This allows for a considerable amount of flexibility in the abdomen as a whole, a feature which is particularly useful during pairing and when the female is egg-laying. The reproductive tissues are harboured inside the abdomen, as is the major part of the digestive tract.

As its name implies, the queen butterfly (Danaus gilippus) *is a relative of the familiar North American monarch. The family Danaidae, to which they both belong, has many representatives in the tropical regions of the world.*

These Jersey tiger moths (Callimorpha quadripunctaria) *have gathered in the inappropriately named 'Valley of the Butterflies' on the Greek island of Rhodes. During the heat of the Mediterranean summer they find refuge in this shady, damp setting.*

Vital Functions

Insects lack a true circulatory system comprising arteries and veins and instead have blood surrounding and bathing the internal organs. Occupying a large volume within is the digestive system, which, in a butterfly or moth, performs essentially the same function as our own. Food—in the case of these insects, in liquid form—is taken in by the mouth and digested within the stomach. Useful nutrition is absorbed into the blood and can be stored as fatty tissue while waste products are passed along the gut and excreted. Waste products in the blood are removed by Malpighian tubules in a way similar to that of our own kidneys. Reproductive organs either produce eggs in females or sperm in males.

Like other insects, butterflies and moths do not possess lungs and instead breathe through a network of tubes called tracheae. These penetrate deep inside the body of the insect, allowing gas exchange to take place and are open to the air via holes called spiracles. There are two pairs of spiracles on the thorax and six to eight pairs on the abdomen in adult butterflies and moths; they are most easily seen, however, along the sides of caterpillars, in particular those of hawkmoths.

This yellow butterfly (Eurema hecabe) is a member of the family Pieridae, commonly known as whites and sulphurs. The genus is widespread in South America, favouring flowery settings such as gardens and areas of regrowth.

The tiger swallowtail (Papilio glaucus) occurs throughout most of North America. During dry spells butterflies gather at pools and puddles where they drink water and imbibe nutrients and salts.

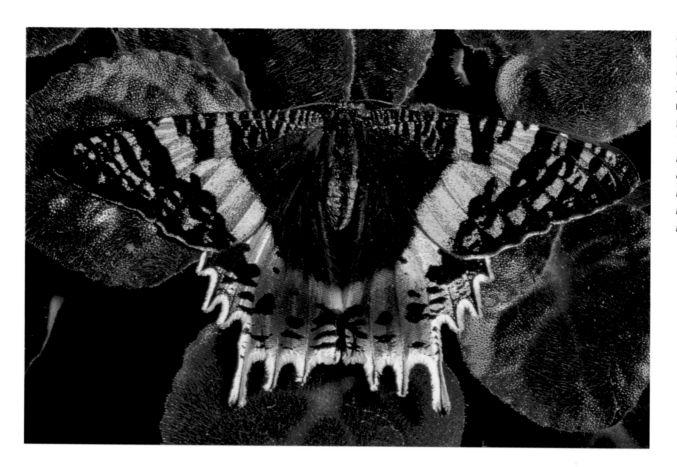

Looking more like a swallowtail butterfly, this sunset moth (Urania ripheus) comes from Madagascar. The family to which it belongs is mainly a tropical one in which most members have iridescent wings.

The greenish marbling on the underside of the hindwing of this orange tip (Anthocharis cardamines) is almost as attractive as the colours on its fore-wings. At rest amongst dappled foliage, they afford the insect surprisingly good camouflage.

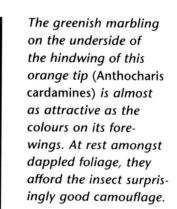

Recently emerged from its pupa, this small elephant hawkmoth (Dielephila porcellus) is resting while its wings dry and harden. The moth gains its English name from the shape of its larva, the head-end of which fancifully re-sembles an elephant's trunk.

THE POWER OF FLIGHT

Without doubt the wings of butterflies and moths are their true glory as seen by human eyes, and also the key to the success of this amazingly diverse group of insects. With them comes the power of flight which for many species is not just assisted gliding but powerful and uninhibited movement through the air. Wings also serve a number of other functions. Striking and often colourful patterns can in some cases advertise a species' identity, or in others help disguise it. Eyespots can startle or deter would-be predators, or provide a relatively harmless target for attack. In addition to these functions, wings provide a stunning and varied celebration of the amazing range of nature's colours.

Wing Structure

Butterfly and moth wings are thin membranous structures that gain rigidity partly by being hardened or chitinised but more importantly by being supported by a network of rigid, hollow veins. The arrangement of these veins is unique to each species, and members of the same family share sufficient similarities in vein structure for this to be a useful feature in taxonomy. Like the other parts of the wings, the veins start out as soft, flaccid structures when the insect emerges from its pupa. They are pumped full of blood and help to expand the wings, drying and hardening in their final position.

Scaly Surface

Butterfly and moth wings are covered with a coating of tiny scales, arranged and overlapping in a manner similar to tiles on the roof of a house. Each one is shaped

Following page: Looking more like a stained-glass window than a butterfly wing, the colours on the hindwing of this giant swallowtail (Papilio cresphontes) are truly amazing. Look closely and you will see the tiny scales which coat the wing surface.

This aptly named blue nymph (Mesosemia croseus) is found in the rain forests of the Amazon basin in Brazil. The amazing blue colour of the wings is caused by the tiny scales that coat them.

Tropical butterflies such as this clearwing butterfly from the West Indies are often very brightly coloured. Butterflies from warm climates, as compared to species from temperate regions, are often rather long-lived.

something like a tennis racket, the 'handle' end attached to the wing itself. In most species of butterfly and moth, it is the scales that are responsible for the colours of the wings. Each scale is stained with pigments produced mainly as by-products of metabolism in the larval and pupal stages. It should also be noted that the scales are loosely attached to the wings and rub off with wear and tear. In some species of butterfly, such as the false Apollo *(Archon apollinus)*, and in moths such as clearwings or the broad-bordered bee hawkmoth *(Hemaris fuciformis)*, large areas of the wings either lose scales or have none in the first place; as the name of the latter species aptly tells us, the resulting appearance is more that of a bee than a moth.

Wing Patterns and Colours

The patterns and colours on the wings of butterflies and moths are so complex and varied as to almost defy belief. The most striking examples are undoubtedly found in the day-flying butterflies, where every colour in the rainbow can be observed in one species or another.

The most intricate and pleasing patterns are found in the swallowtails and their allies. Species such as the European swallowtail *(Papilio machaon)*, tiger swallowtail *(Papilio glaucus)*, or southern festoon *(Zerynthia polyxena)*, have patterns resembling stained-glass windows. Close contenders for winners in this natural beauty contest can be found amongst the nymphalid butterflies, whose tropical representatives have patterns of blue, yellow, red, and orange. Even temperate nymphalid species such as the painted lady *(Vanessa cardui)*, small tortoiseshell *(Aglais urticae)*, or Camberwell beauty, mourning cloak *(Nymphalis antiopa)*, are stunning to look at.

Birds are consistent predators of insects and, not surprisingly, many butterfly species

Famed for the power and distance of its migratory flights, the monarch butterfly (Danaus plexippus) *is widespread in North America during the summer months. In the winter large numbers gather in the milder climate of the southern United States and Central America.*

This is a rusty-tipped butterfly (Siproeta epaphus), *photographed in Mexico. The wealth of butterfly species exhibit a bewildering range of colours and patterns whose specific functions often elude scientists.*

Swallowtails belong to the family Papilionidae and include some of the most attractive of all butterflies. This giant swallowtail (Papilio cresphontes) *is basking in the sun, its backlit wings providing a most impressive sight.*

These attractive butterflies (Urania leila) *are members of the family Uraniidae, although they superficially resemble swallowtails. They come from the Rondonia region of Brazil, and are here imbibing salts from a muddy patch on the forest floor.*

There can be few more convincing examples of camouflage than that of this insect. Until it moves, this Indian leaf butterfly (Kallima paralekta) *looks for all the world like a dry leaf.*

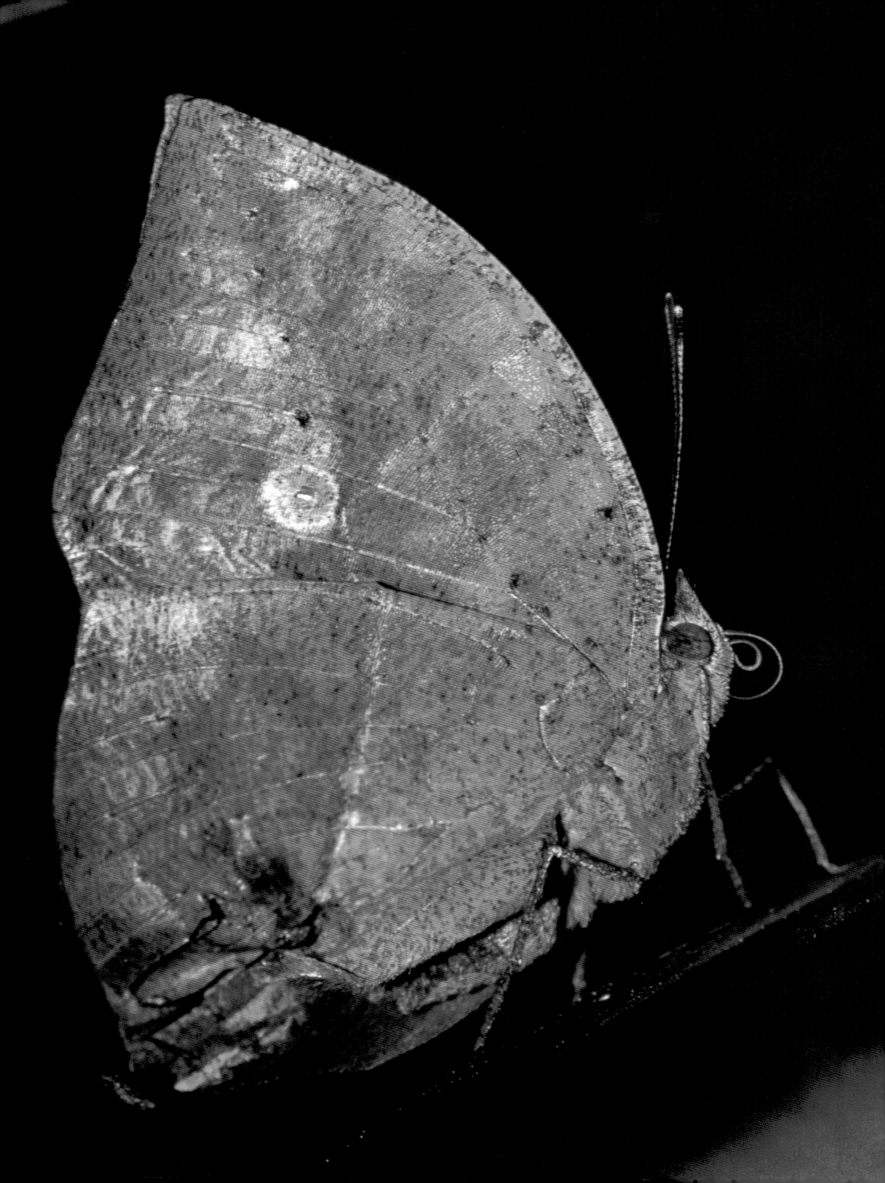

go out of their way to avoid being caught, either by utilising rapid flight or cryptic colouring when at rest. At first glance it is perhaps curious, therefore, that some appear to advertise their presence. Many tropical butterflies, as well as the North American monarch butterfly *(Danaus plexippus)*, have brightly coloured wings and confident flight. This is because their bodies have accumulated toxins from larval foodplants such as, in the case of the monarch, milkweed. Birds learn to recognise the markings and associate them with unpleasant tastes. Avoidance behaviour then follows.

Hidden Meaning

Being largely nocturnal, moths have little need for vivid wing patterns; more important is the need for camouflage while resting during the daytime. Not surprisingly, many species, such as the mottled beauty *(Alcis repandata)*, have wings that are remarkably like tree bark and they use these markings to good effect. Others have more specific patterns and wing shapes. For instance, the buff tip *(Phalera bucephala)* resembles a piece of chipped birch bark or twig, while the lappet moth *(Gastropacha quercifolia)* bears a striking resemblance to a dead beech leaf.

Some moths not only have wings with camouflage markings but also adopt postures that heighten the deception. This moth from the Amazon rain forest closely resembles a broken piece of twig.

The mottled brown and pinkish buff markings on the wings of this rain-forest hawkmoth from Ecuador provide superb camouflage as it rests on lichen-covered tree bark.

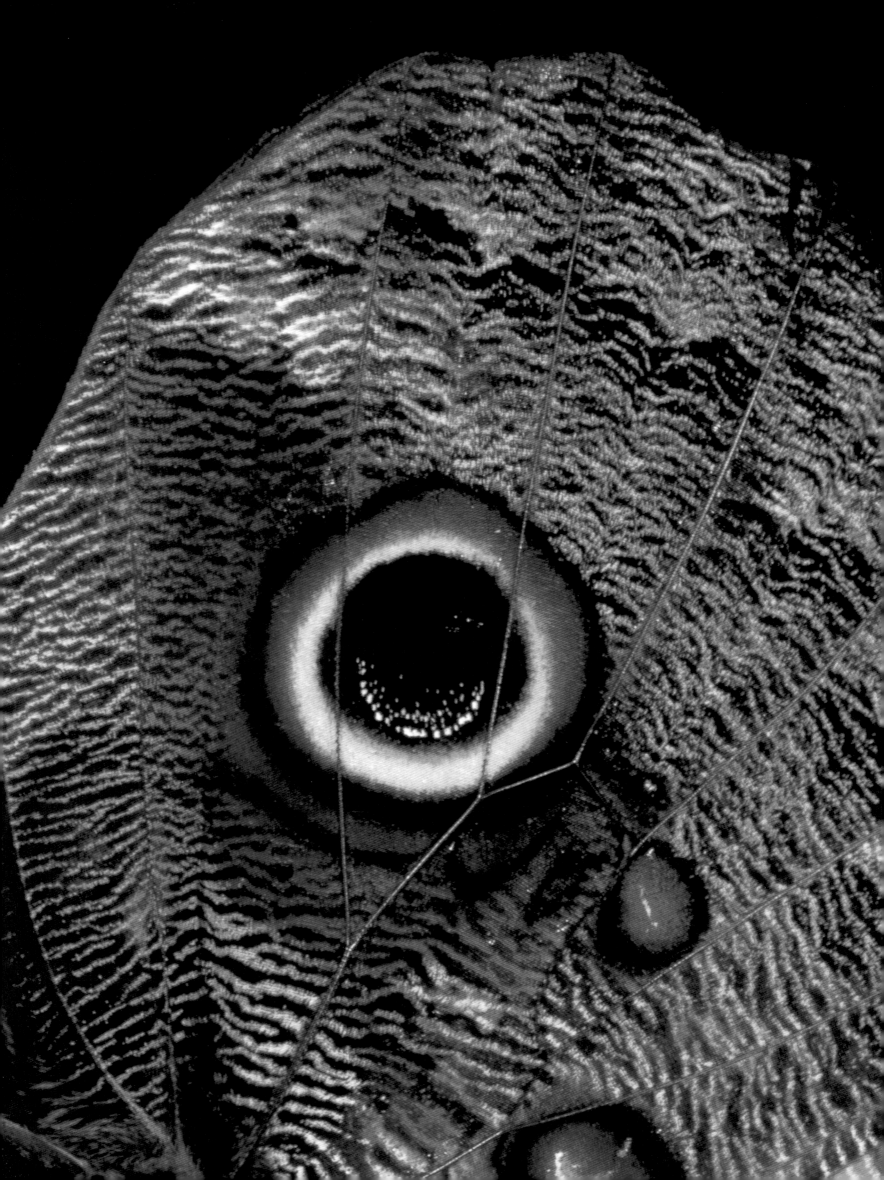

Eyespots

One of the most frequently encountered wing markings in both butterflies and moths is the eye marking. Apart from being merely decorative, these would appear to serve two purposes, both of which have to do with predation. Firstly, they can serve as false eyes, attracting the attention of would-be predators who then attack this 'eye' and instead get a mouthful of wing—better to lose a section of wing, naturally, than the head itself. The second purpose would appear to be one of startling an attacker. This is perhaps seen to best effect in the eyed hawkmoth *(Smerinthus ocellatus)*. At rest the bark-patterned forewings cover the hindwings, giving the insect a cryptic appearance. When alarmed, however, the hindwings are exposed to reveal two large and impressive 'eyes'; the effect is further enhanced by the creature's thrusting these so-called eyes toward the attacker.

How Flight is Achieved

The fore- and hindwings of butterflies and moths are not fused in any way, as is the case with some other groups of insects. They do, however, in most species overlap and have coupling devices. In flight they beat in harmony with one another. By a combination of powerful muscles contracting within the thorax and an intriguing mechanical distortion

Long tail streamers on the hindwings characterise moths of the genus Argema. This individual (Argema maenas), which has a wingspan of 13 centimetres (5 inches), is found in the tropical forests of Sumatra.

of the thorax itself, the wings flap up and down several times a second. As a consequence of this ability, butterflies and moths are capable of attaining speeds of between 8 to 17 kilometres per hour (5 to 10 miles per hour), depending on the species; some butterflies and moths can even hover.

Flight Patterns

Just as wing size varies tremendously amongst butterflies and moths, so too does

The plain, cryptic colouring on the underwings of this comma butterfly (Polygonia c-album) contrast markedly with the attractive, tawny-brown upperwings. This individual is sunbathing, a favourite occupation of the species.

The markings which give the owl butterfly (Caligo eurilochus) its name bear more than a passing resemblance to staring eyes. The effect is useful enough to frighten off most potential predators.

When resting or sunbathing, butterflies usually hold their wings out flat and spread them, as can be seen with this Smyrna butterfly (Smyrna blomfildia), photographed in Ecuador.

Butterfly wings vary considerably in size and shape, depending on the species. In general, however, the forewings are usually rather pointed at the tip while the hindwings are rounded, as can be seen in this Ecuadorian species (Adelpha oytherea).

The upperwings of the red admiral (Vanessa atalanta) are striking and distinctive. This wide-ranging butterfly occurs across much of temperate North America as well as in Europe and North Africa.

The marbled undersides of the red admiral's (Vanessa atalanta) hindwings afford it excellent camouflage when resting or feeding on flowers. The undersides of the forewings show a hint of the splendour of their upper surfaces.

the way in which they fly. Indeed, some have such characteristic flight patterns that experienced entomologists can even identify specific species on the wing with a degree of certainty.

Butterflies such as the iridescent morphos of the South American rain forests have extremely powerful flight and can easily outpace most would-be predators. With their broad wings they are capable of long glides and are extremely elegant. By contrast, many of the smaller forest species, such as the postman butterfly (Heliconius melpomone), have comparatively weak, fluttery flight; this type of flight is shared by many temperate species, such as the wood white (Leptidea sinapis). It is a wonder sometimes, seeing this latter species in flight, that it ever gets airborne.

Other species of butterfly will only fly at certain times of day or under certain condi-

tions. Some of the tropical owl butterflies will fly only at dusk, while mountain or alpine butterflies take to the wing only during spells of sunshine, dropping like stones to the ground the instant a cloud obscures the sun.

Many smaller species of moths have a somewhat buzzing flight during which it is difficult to make out the wings as anything other than a blur. The same can be said for skipper butterflies, which have many moth-like characteristics. A feature of the flight of many moths but of fewer butterflies is the ability to hover for extended periods. Particularly adept at this are the hawkmoths, which habitually remain motionless in front of nectar-rich flowers while feeding with their long, extended tongues.

Butterfly Migration

Some butterflies and moths move only relatively short distances during their lives. For example, the speckled wood (Pararge aegeria), similar to that of many rain-forest species, are faithful to a single, specific clearing or glade. Others, however, are more wide ranging and fly long distances. The movements of some species, such as the death's-head hawkmoth (Acherontia atropos), silvery moth (Autographa gamma), or painted lady (Vanessa cardui), are best described as dispersive rather than migratory. Each spring or summer, successive broods move farther and farther north, following the progression of the seasons.

A few butterflies do, however, perform migrations in the strict meaning of the word. That is they not only move in one direction toward breeding grounds, but also move in the reverse direction later in the year. The most well-known example of this, of course, is the monarch butterfly, which winters in the southern United States and Mexico but moves north in the spring, some even spreading into Canada. The flight distances involved for these butterflies can exceed 3,000 kilometres (1,800 miles).

THE WEALTH OF SPECIES

Scientists arrange the huge diversity of butterfly and moth species into families, and although there is no distinct difference in classification terms between the two groups of insects, for the purposes of this book they are considered as separate from one another. Depending on the authority referred to, the Lepidoptera comprise as many as seventy different families, only a few of which are butterflies (experts argue as to whether there are just six butterfly families or whether they should be subdivided further). Although many of the moth families in particular are represented by tiny or obscure species there are nevertheless tens of thousands of attractive examples. With a book of this size, only a selection of the larger and more impressive species can be included and the families discussed below are a small but representative selection of the full range.

Swallowtails

These butterflies belong to the family Papilionidae and include some of the largest and most impressive of all species. Many are brightly coloured and representatives are found in most parts of the world.

The family name derives from a characteris-

The great Victorian explorer Alfred Russel Wallace discovered the croseus birdwing butterfly (Ornithoptera croseus) on an expedition to the Malay peninsula in 1859. It is one of the largest butterflies in the world with a wingspan in excess of 15 centimetres (6 inches).

These Japanese swallowtails (Papilio xuthus) have extremely intricate markings on their wings. Their patterns are not simply for show but serve as an important stimulus during courtship.

The giant swallowtail (Papilio cresphontes) is widespread in the southern United States. This powerful flier lays its eggs on citrus trees and the resulting caterpillars, which have orange scented protuberances, are known locally as 'orange dogs'.

tic shared by many of the true swallowtails, that is, the presence of tail streamers on the hindwing. In species such as the European swallowtail *(Papilio machaon)* or the zebra swallowtail *(Papilio marcellus),* there is one tail streamer of moderate length per hindwing. In some tropical swallowtails there are two or more streamers, and they can be extremely long. The caterpillars of swallowtails are often brightly coloured and can expand a strong-smelling protuberance—the osmaterium—used to deter predators.

The most spectacular members of the swallowtail family are without doubt the birdwing butterflies, found mainly in Southeast Asia. These huge and impressive insects, some with wingspans of 20 centimetres (8 inches) or more, are residents of rain-forest tree canopies and seldom, if ever, descend to ground level. Early collectors had to resort to shooting them with fine shot since netting them was out of the question.

Apollo butterflies *(Parnassius spp.)* are also members of the swallowtail family. Several different species are known and they occur mainly in mountainous regions of Europe. They are large and rather docile insects that are fond of sunning themselves on flower heads, particularly during the early morning or late evening. Their wings often look waxy with age and become worn-looking through loss of scales. The caterpillars of Apollo butterflies are strangely plump and feed mainly on the leaves of houseleeks and stonecrops.

Skippers

The skippers are an aptly named group of butterflies whose flight can indeed be likened to skipping or darting. They belong to the family Hesperiidae and, in many ways, are mothlike in character, since they often rest with their wings out flat or at least partly so. Most skipper species are rather small and dull in appearance, especially those from temperate regions of the world. Those from the tropics, however, can be brightly coloured, and achieve wingspans of 5 centimetres (2 inches) or more. Several species of skippers are found at high altitudes or at cold latitudes. In the European Alps, for example, the alpine grizzled skipper *(Pyrgus andromedae)* flies at altitudes of 3,500 metres (11,550 feet) or more, while in North America the Arctic skipper (in Europe, called the chequered skipper) tolerates prolonged and bitter winters in its early stages.

Raja Brook's bird-wing (Trogonoptera brookiana) *is one of the most wide-spread of the bird-wing butterflies. It occurs in many parts of Malaysia, and although it is mainly found high in the tree canopy it will occasionally descend to the forest floor to drink.*

The plain tiger (Danaus chrysippus) *is a relative of the more familiar monarch butterfly. It occurs in both Africa and Asia, and in the former is mimicked by the mocker swallowtail* (Papilio dardanus). *The swallowtail gains protection from the deception since predators avoid the plain tiger's unpleasant taste.*

Whites

The whites belong to the family Pieridae and have representatives in most parts of the world. Some are extremely common and a few are notorious pests of man's crops, the damage done during their larval stages.

The small white *(Pieris rapae)* is a widespread species in Europe and one which is distinctly unpopular with gardeners and farmers alike. The eggs are laid on leaves of the cabbage family and can strip plants bare; not surprisingly, its alternative common name is the cabbage white. In the mid-1800s the small white was introduced into North America and is now as widespread and reviled there as in its native region.

As their name relates, a notable feature of many members of the white family is their white wings. Veins, however, are often outlined with darker scaling, and a particularly attractive example is seen in the green-veined white *(Pieris napi)*—known in North America as the mustard white. The black-veined white *(Aporia crataegi)* has wings that are almost translucent.

Splashes of colour are also not uncommon in this group and a particularly attractive example is the orange tip *(Anthocharis cardamines)* of Europe, or the falcate orange tip *(Anthocharis genutia)* of North America, the males of which have striking orange tips to their upper forewings. The Pieridae also include strikingly colourful butterflies known as brimstones and sulphurs, whose wings are dominated by yellow and orange hues. The brimstone *(Gonepteryx rhamni)* has strangely curved and angled wings which, at rest, can resemble the undersides of leaves. A two-brooded butterfly found in Europe, the brimstone hibernates through the winters, seemingly unaffected by cold weather. The common sulphur *(Colias philodice)* of North America and its equivalent, the clouded yellow *(Colias crocea)* of Europe, are strong-flying butterflies that favour feeding on alfalfa, a larval foodplant. The former species has a predilection for drinking at

Bright yellow is a common colour amongst members of the family Pieridae, whose species are sometimes known as whites and sulphurs. Photographed here is a little yellow (Eurema lisa) *from Central America.*

44

puddles, a habit shared by many tropical members of the Pieridae, who can sometimes be seen gathered by the hundreds at muddy pool margins.

Blues, Coppers, and Hairstreaks

Although most members of the wide-ranging family Lycaenidae are comparatively small, this is made up for by the striking colours and patterns or the unusual shapes of their wings. Many are engagingly active butterflies and some have fascinating life histories.

As their common name denotes, many of the blues do indeed have blue upperwings, although these are more commonly seen in males than in females, which are often brown. The range of hues extends from purplish or chalky blue to almost iridescent, as can be seen in the Adonis blue *(Lysandra bellargus)*. Several species of blues exhibit larval associations with ants. In the chalk-hill blue *(Lysandra coridon)*, the larvae produce a honeydewlike secretion and are 'milked' by ants in their later stages. From this symbiotic relationship the ants derive nutrition and the larvae gain a degree of protection from

invertebrate predators. In the large blue *(Maculinea arion)*, this relationship is taken one stage further. In its last stage, the larva is carried underground by ants where it spends its days feeding on their grubs.

Coppers are an attractive group of butterflies with upperwings in many of the species that are metallic-orange in appearance.

A male orange tip (Anthocharis cardamines) rests on leaves of dog mercury in a Sussex woodland. As soon as a female appears, he will pursue her in an attempt to initiate courtship. She will lay her eggs on cuckooflower.

Idas blue butterflies (Lucaeides idas) can be found in many parts of western Europe. Those at high altitudes tend to be smaller in size than others in lower, warmer areas.

Hairstreaks, on the other hand, often have rather sombrely coloured upperwings. The underwings, however, are usually delicately marked and bear streaklike markings, from which they get their name; the hindwings usually bear prominent, and sometimes long, tail streamers.

Nymphalids

Members of the large family Nymphalidae are varied both in terms of size and appearance, and number amongst some of the most colourful and attractive of all butterfly species. Nymphalids occur in most parts of the world and can be found flying in habitats ranging from the Arctic tundra to tropical rain forests.

The fritillaries are amongst the more readily identifiable and attractive nymphalids. Most have orange-brown wings with dark spots and squares, frequently giving a chequerboard appearance; the underwings are often marked with silvery white spots. Some fritillaries are rather sluggish fliers while others, such as the Queen of Spain fritillary (*Issoria lathonia*), have a powerful flight and sometimes cover long distances.

Copper butterflies are in fact relatives of the blues, both members of the family Lycaenidae. This purple-edged copper (Palaeochry-sophanus hippothoe), photographed in France, is one of the larger and more showy examples.

Tail streamers on the hindwings characterise the group of butterflies commonly known as hairstreaks. This regal hairstreak (Evernus regalis) from Mexico is a particularly fine example, with colourful wings and long 'tails'.

Orange-brown wings are typical of fritillary butterflies. Species such as this Queen of Spain (Issoria lathonia), with relatively pointed forewings, are fast fliers.

The small tortoiseshell (Aglais urticae) is widespread and particularly common in Europe. The adult butterfly hibernates during the winter months, often moving indoors to do so.

The nymphalids that occur in the tropics include some of the most colourful of all butterflies and a few have considerable wingspans. Almost every conceivable colour can be found here in one species or another and the variety of wing shapes is seemingly limitless.

In temperate regions, several species of nymphalids hibernate as adults during the winter months. These include the Camberwell beauty, or mourning cloak (*Nymphalis antiopa*), small tortoiseshell (*Aglais urticae*), and the peacock (*Nymphalis io*). Other interesting temperate species include the map butterfly (*Araschnia levana*), whose wings bear intricate maplike markings, the two-tailed pashsa (*Charaxes jasius*), whose hindwings bear swallowtail-like streamers, and the purple emperor (*Apatura iris*), the males of which have a magnificent purple sheen on their upperwings.

Browns

While there are some extremely colourful members of the family Satyridae, the majority are adequately described by these butterflies' common generic name. Many do, however, show subtle but beautiful marbling and patterning on the underwings, and a feature common to many species is the presence of eyespots on the wings.

Temperate species are often associated with open spaces, meadows, and grassy woodland rides since the larval foodplants are usually varieties of grasses. Some species

Butterflies belonging to the genus Callicore *are widespread in South America and belong to the family Nymphalidae. This species is imaginatively called the '88' butterfly, after the markings on its hindwings.*

Known in Britain as the Camberwell beauty and in North America as the mourning cloak, this species (Nymphalis antiopa) *is an attractive member of the family Nymphalidae. It is widespread in temperate regions of the northern hemisphere.*

This malachite butterfly (Sippoeta stelenes) *is a member of the family Nymphalidae. Its distribution includes many parts of Central America that experience tropical or sub-tropical climates.*

Famous for its remarkable eyespot markings, the peacock butterfly (Inachus io) *is widespread in Europe. The false eyes serve to distract predators, thus reducing the risk of damage in the event of an attack.*

Butterfly wings are membranous and are supported by a network of rigid veins. On the orange-brown wings of this gulf fritillary these can be clearly seen outlined in black.

A lover of dry, sunny slopes, the wall brown (Lasiommata megera) is a widespread butterfly in Europe, and can often be seen sunbathing on paths or walls. There is considerable variation in ground colour across its range; southern specimens are much paler than this example.

are even territorial. Males of the North American pearly eye *(Lethe portlandia)* adopt a favoured tree in a clearing from which they can spy on other males; when sighted they are chased away with an aggression surprising for a butterfly. In a similar way, male speckled woods *(Pararge aegeria)* perch on sprays of leaves where they can survey their own sunny clearing. If another male strays too close he is driven away after a spiraling duel—careful study has revealed that the occupying male invariably wins these contests.

The cardinal butterfly (Pandoriana pandora) is a member of the group commonly known as fritillaries. It is an active insect found in warmer parts of mainland Europe and has upperwings that are fulvous brown.

Tropical Specialists

Although some families of butterflies have representatives throughout the world, several are specific to warm, tropical regions with few, or in some cases, no species occurring elsewhere. Perhaps the best known of these are the morpho butterflies (family Morphidae), many species of which are famous for their stunning metallic-blue upperwings. They are found only in the tropical forests of Central and South America, and visitors to these regions will fast become familiar with the sight of these magnificent insects gliding with ease and grace amongst the higher reaches of the tree canopy.

This same region of the world also boasts a wide range of owl butterflies (family Brassolidae), so-called because of the striking owl 'eyes' on the underside of many of the species hindwings. Rather curiously, some of the larger and more spectacular species have hindwings that are larger than

A Julia butterfly (Dryas julia) from Central America feeds on a flower. Like many other tropical species, it too gathers in groups on riverbanks to imbibe salts and nutrients from the damp soil.

Occurring in places as wide ranging as central Mexico and Ecuador, this rare blue doctor (Rhetus arcius) is a rain-forest species. The tail streamers on its hindwings recall those of swallowtail butterflies.

Heliconid butterflies are widespread in Central and South America. Many, such as this species (Heliconius aoede), are brightly coloured, advertising the fact that they are distasteful to would-be predators such as birds.

This lesser purple emperor (Apatura ilia) *and its close relative the purple emperor* (Apatura iris) *are the nearest thing to morpho butterflies that occur in Europe. The metallic-purple sheen is only seen in males, and even then only when the angle of light on the wings is correct.*

their forewings, and both are fantastically marked and patterned to resemble tree bark. In the forests of Southeast Asia, where owl butterflies and morphos are absent, they are replaced by the family Amathusiidae, whose members often look superficially similar to their South American counterparts.

Although much smaller, the heliconid butterflies (family Heliconiidae) are also very familiar and widespread throughout South and Central America, the range of a few species extending somewhat into the southern portion of the United States. What they lack in size they make up for with an attractive array of colourful wings. All are fairly similar in shape, possessing narrow and elongated wings, particularly the forewings. Although their flight is rather weak, they are seldom taken by birds because of their unpalatable taste, as their bright colours advertise. The metalmark butterflies (family Nemeobiidae), although similarly small, are far from uniform in shape. They exhibit almost as many variations as it is possible to imagine, and are perhaps the most colourful group of butterflies when taken as a whole.

Before butterfly collecting was considered politically incorrect, the metallic-blue morpho butterflies, such as this species (Morpho peleides), *were amongst the most highly prized of all specimens. The group is wide ranging in the rain forests of Central and South America.*

Owl butterflies such as this example (Caligo memnon) *are widespread in tropical regions of Central and South America. The owl-like appearance suggested by the false eyes is further enhanced by the delicate scaling on the rest of the wings, which fancifully resembles feathering.*

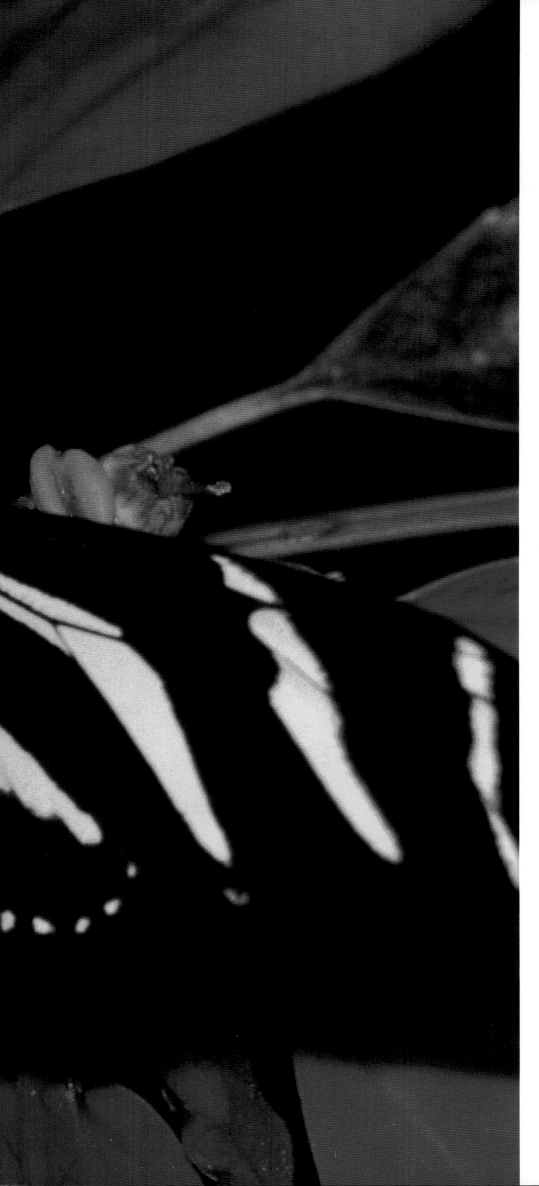

Underwing markings on this many-banded dagger-wing (Marpesia chiron) give the insect its common name. The butterfly comes from the rain forests of Ecuador. Males have striking blue-green iridescent upperwings.

This attractive little butterfly (Anteros acheus) comes from Ecuador. It belongs to the family Nemeobiidae, or metalmarks, a group which is diverse in tropical regions of the world.

The zebra (Heliconius charitonius) comes from forests in Mexico. It roosts communally at night, which is unusual for butterflies. The insects are protected by their unpleasant smell and taste, common to all members of the genus.

Burnet Moths

The burnet moths are an interesting group of day-flying moths belonging to the family Zygaenidae and are particularly well represented in Europe. They are usually brightly coloured, red and blue-black the most frequently seen, and make no attempt to conceal themselves while feeding on flower heads. The bright markings advertise the fact that they are unpleasant tasting and birds soon learn to attribute this fact to them.

Pyralid and Plume Moths

Although belonging to separate families, the pyralid moths (family Pyralidae) and the plume moths (family Pterophoridae) are often studied together. They represent a large number of small moths, some of which are extremely common and can be agricultural pests. Some pyralid moths are colourful but most are fairly dull in appearance. The larvae of some species are found in unusual habitats, feeding on seemingly unlikely foods. The wax moth *(Galleria mellonella)*, for example, has larvae that feed on bees wax in hives and can cause considerable damage. Other species feed on flour or create galls, while the larvae of the brown china mark moth

The luna moth (Actius luna) *is surely one of North America's most spectacular species, characterised by the long streamers on its hindwings. Note the large, feathery antennae used by males to detect the scent of females.*

The staring eyespots on the hindwings of this North American io moth are its most striking feature. Normally hidden by the forewings when at rest, the 'eyes' are revealed when danger threatens.

(Nymphula nympheata) are aquatic and make cases from portions of water plant leaves. The plume moths, by contrast, are best known for their appearance as adults; the wings are highly divided and look for all the world like feather plumes.

Geometrids

Adults of the family Geometridae are extremely varied and it is difficult to find unifying characteristics to link them together. When it comes to the larvae, however, it is easier to find commonalities. They are elongated and walk characteristically by looping their bodies; this gives rise to their common names of 'looper caterpillars', in Britain, and 'inchworms', as they are known in the United States. Many of them are camouflaged to resemble twigs and adopt a posture on their foodplant that enhances the deception.

Atlas and Silk Moths

Members of the family Saturniidae include some of the largest moths in the world. The atlas moth *(Attacus atlas)* from Southeast Asia, for example, has a wingspan that can exceed 30 centimetres (12 inches). Many species also have incredible patterns on their wings, including well-developed eyespots, as seen in the emperor moth *(Pavonia pavonia)* of Europe and the bull's-eye moth *(Automeris io)* of North America. Equally attractive and impressive are North America's robin moth *(Hyalophora cecropia)* and the Indian moon moth *(Actias selene)*, the latter possessing subtle green wings and elegant tail streamers. Many of the Saturniidae are referred to as silk moths, as the pupae are surrounded by hardened silken cocoons. The true silk moth, *Bombyx mori*, however, belongs to the Bombycidae, a closely related family.

Hawkmoths

Hawkmoths belong to the family Sphingidae and are wide ranging throughout the world. Both larvae and adults are easily recognised as belonging to this group, as most species share distinctive characteristics. The adults are in many cases fast-flying; they have streamlined bodies and relatively narrow wings designed for speed and hovering. This latter ability enables members of the

Silk moths and their relatives number amongst some of the largest and most attractive of all moths. This yellow emperor moth is surely a good example and comes from the forests of Borneo.

Atlas moths are members of the family Saturniidae and number amongst some of the largest moths in the world. This species was photographed in South America and has a wingspan in excess of 23 centimetres (9 inches).

group, notably the convolvulus hawkmoth *(Agrius convolvuli)*, to feed on the wing, utilising its long and well-developed proboscis for the purpose. Some hawkmoths are capable of long-distance flights. Southern Europe, for example, is rich in hawkmoth species and, in good years, many of these move northward. There are regular records of death's-head hawkmoths *(Acherontia atropos)*, spurge hawkmoths *(Hyles euphorbiae)*, and hummingbird hawkmoths *(Macroglossum stellatarum)* occurring as far north as Britain. Hawkmoth caterpillars, although varied in colour and size, invariably show a marked 'horn' at the tail end. Many species are beautifully marked and bear oblique stripes along the body, rendering suitable camouflage while feeding.

Prominents

Prominents belong to the family Notodontidae, another wide-ranging group of moths. Many species exhibit remarkable camouflage when at rest during the daytime and, in profile, show characteristic humps or 'prominences' on the head and thorax, from which their common name derives. Prominent larvae often have strange appearances, none more so than that of the lobster moth *(Stauropus fagi)*, which fancifully resembles a lobster, or more realistically a praying mantis, when at rest.

Hawkmoths are often referred to as sphinx moths in North America, where the group is diverse and often common. This Xylophanes *species is an active, fast-flying moth.*

Few guesses are needed as to how the death's-head hawkmoth (Acherontia atropos) *gets its name. As if the skull and crossbones marking on its thorax were not sufficient deterrent, the moth also squeaks loudly if disturbed.*

Many resemble tree bark while others can resemble dead leaves.

Tiger Moths

Some members of the family Actiidae might be more appropriately named leopard moths instead of tiger moths since the wing markings are often broken up into blotches and spots rather than stripes. Many members of the group are strikingly marked and some are very colourful, an appearance that sometimes reflects the fact that they are distasteful to predators. Warning colours are of little use after dark to ward off moths' main predators—bats—and some species have learnt to use the bats' echolocation to their own advantage. A few species can detect bat ultrasound and take avoiding action, while others can actually emit their own ultrasounds, in effect jamming the bats' means of detection. In general adult moths are rather solitary creatures. Unusually, however, the Jersey tiger moth (*Callimorpha quadripunctaria*) of Europe gathers in huge hordes in certain parts of its range. In particular, tens of thousands of these moths gather during the hot summer months at the inappropriately named 'Valley of the Butterflies' on the Mediterranean island of Rhodes. They take advantage of the humidity and cool temperatures at this wooded stream valley.

Noctuids

The Noctuidae family contains the largest number of species of any moth family—more than 20,000 in all. Most are variable in size and shape but almost all have wings that afford them excellent camouflage. When seen out of context, the wing patterns and markings can be beautiful and colourful. When the moth is located in the habitat for which the pattern was designed, the camouflage effect is often astonishing.

Although striking and beautiful when seen up close, this forest moth from the slopes of Mount Kinabalu in Sabah, Malaysia, is a superb leaf-mimic when it rests on the leaf carpet.

The rich colours on the wings of this royal walnut moth (Citheronia regalis) make it one of northern North America's most attractive species as well as one of the largest. Its wing veins can be seen clearly.

BUTTERFLY LIVES

Butterflies and moths offer such a fascinating range of shapes and colours in adult life that this aspect alone can make a worthy study. Take your interest one stage further, however, into life-cycle study, and you will discover much more about their intriguing behaviour.

Butterfly Life Cycle

The life cycle of a butterfly or moth involves four stages: the egg, the larval stage, the pupal stage, and the adult. Unlike some other insects, such as bugs where the stages in the life cycle show a gradual change and acquisition of adult characteristics, those of the butterfly are dramatically different. The transition between the stages involves a process called metamorphosis and it is a truly remarkable natural phenomenon. The different stages in the life cycle last for varying periods of time according to the species involved and its geographical location. In the tropics some species will breed almost continuously, the cycle endlessly repeating itself. In temperate regions the life cycles may be more or less continuous during the summer months or, more often, repeated only on an annual basis.

The Egg

Compared to the adult butterfly or moth, the eggs laid by the female are always relatively small. They are often rounded in shape and can be almost spherical, although in some species they may be cylindrical. The egg comprises a hard outer casing which can be smooth or sculptured with ridges or patterns. Inside, the embryo develops into a miniature larva which eventually darkens the egg just prior to hatching.

Depending on the species, eggs can be laid singly or in batches of ten or more. In most cases they are laid on the leaves of the larval foodplant, which the female had selected with great care. This is particularly vital since many larvae are extremely fussy eaters and will not take anything other than their specific foodplant. The egg stage lasts a varying amount of time depending on the butterfly or moth species involved, although a typical period of time would be from eight to fifteen days.

This caterpillar is protected by a covering of irritating hairs. As a further defence, it lives inside a rolled-up leaf, whose margins bind it together with its own silk.

Some species of butterflies and moths lay their eggs singly. Others, such as the marsh fritillary (Euphydryas aurinia) seen here, are laid in masses on the leaves of a suitable foodplant.

Blue is a colour which is often seen on butterfly upperwings, with examples coming from many butterfly families. It is less frequently observed on their underwings, however, and there can be few more striking examples than this butterfly from Peru.

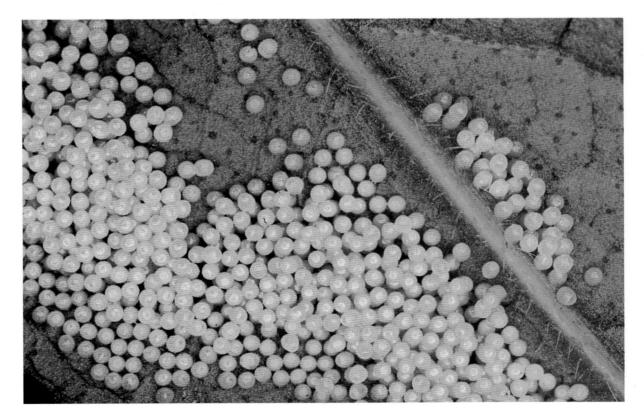

The Larva

Once the tiny larva has emerged from its egg, and in some cases consumed the egg case as its first meal, it can get on with its primary role in life, namely eating and growing. Butterfly and moth larvae are, in the majority of species, vegetarians, eating the leaves of flowering plants. A hardened head and set of mouthparts enable them to tackle the plant tissue, which is then digested by the digestive system lying within the segmented body. Near the head the larva has three pairs of true legs on segments, which correspond to the adult's thorax. At the tail end there are suckerlike false legs that help the creature cling to its food.

Although the body of the larva is relatively soft, there is a limit to how much it can expand as it eats and grows. Periodically, therefore, the larva moults its old skin, which splits at the head end. The larva emerges with a new, softer body that will expand before the new skin hardens. The periods between larval moults are known as instars and, in most cases, the number of instars varies from three to five, depending on the species.

Butterfly and moth larvae vary tremendously in their size and shape. If there were such a thing as a typical larva it would perhaps be long and rather cylindrical with a smooth skin. Not surprisingly, however, the variation amongst larvae is as great as that seen in the adults. Those of geometrid moths, for instance, are often knobbly and elongate, resembling twigs, while those of hairstreak butterflies are squat and flattened. Many larvae are hairy, some in the extreme, while others may be spiky; these are both adaptations to discourage potential predators.

The Pupa

Following the last larval stage, the insect undergoes a dramatic metamorphosis to

Having recently emerged from its pupa, this monarch butterfly (Danaus plexippus) is resting while its wings expand and harden. It may take an hour or so after emergence before it attempts its first flight.

The caterpillars of the large white live in groups on their foodplants, which include members of the cabbage family, or in this case nasturtium. They can completely defoliate a plant in a matter of days.

The body of this cecropia moth larva (Hyalophora cecropia) is covered with tubercles and projections. Its true legs can be seen grasping the stem in close proximity to its head. Larger false legs are seen farther down its body.

become the pupa. Having found a suitable location for pupation, the larval skin splits and from it emerges the pupa, displaying a mixture of both larval and adult characteristics. The head, with its large eyes and proboscis, is usually clearly visible as are the wings and the legs of the adult butterfly or moth.

Pupae are found in a variety of settings. Many moth pupae are found underground; the larva had burrowed there prior to pupation. Normally, a pupation chamber is excavated and this often has its walls lined with silk. Pupae that are found above ground are often protected by a much more considerable silken cocoon. Butterfly pupae are sometimes found amongst vegetation at ground level or on the larval foodplants. In many species the pupa is attached in some way to its chosen pupation substrate via silk.

The duration of the pupal stage can vary from a couple of weeks in some tropical species to more than nine months in temperate ones where overwintering occurs. During this time the organs and tissues of the larva reform to become those of the adult, with new features such as wings and wing muscles appearing.

These paired sara orange tip butterflies (Anthocharis sara) are resting unobtrusively amongst vegetation. They are vulnerable to attack by predators at this time since their ability to fly is rather restricted.

Metalmark butterflies are an intriguing group belonging to the family Riodinidae which, at first glance, may resemble day-flying moths. Pointed tips of the clubbed antennae are characteristic, as can be seen in this species (Apodemia palmeri).

Powerful suckers on the false legs of this cecropia moth larva (Hyalophora cecropia) are the primary means by which the insect holds onto its foodplant. Most larvae have five pairs of these false legs.

Following page: Pairing in butterflies and moths can sometimes last for several hours. During this time the tips of the abdomen remain linked to ensure successful fertilisation. This can be seen clearly with these promethea moths.

The Adult

To witness the emergence of a butterfly from its pupa is one of the true wonders of nature. For a day or so prior to emergence, the form of the adult can often be seen through the pupal casing and indeed the colours of the wings are sometimes visible too. The process of emergence involves the head end of the pupa splitting, the result of the adult inside inflating this part of its body. The mature insect drags itself out of the casing with its wings damp and flaccid. Blood is pumped into the wing veins and once the wings have fully expanded they begin to dry. An hour or so later the insect can attempt its first flight.

Rearing Butterflies and Moths

With a few exceptions, butterflies and moths are comparatively easy to rear through their entire life cycle as long as you pay heed to the needs of the different stages. Butterflies and moths usually lay their eggs on the preferred foodplant of the larva and this is what should be used in all cases. Ensure that fresh leaves are always available and that larval droppings are removed regularly. Some people prefer to rear larvae on vegetation with the stems in water to keep the leaves fresh. This method can, however, lead to problems, and a well-ventilated plastic tub is often the best container.

The two worst factors affecting larval survival are overheating and high humidity.

When a larva is ready to pupate it will usually give you a few clues as to its intentions. It will stop eating and often change colour in some way. Lastly it might go on a walkabout, looking for the ideal spot for pupation. Make sure you know the requirements of the species involved: some like to bury themselves in several inches of soil, others prefer leaf litter or may want to attach themselves to a plant stem. If in doubt, give them all the options. Pupae should be kept in a cool place where they are free from frost, excessive dampness, or heat. A few twigs should be placed in the container for the emerging adult to climb upon in order to dry its wings.

Moth Trapping

As day-flying insects, butterflies are comparatively easy to see, but moths, which are largely nocturnal, present more of a problem in terms of observation. During the daytime most moths remain hidden and are difficult to locate. One way of seeing a vast range of moths is to use a mercury vapour lamp to attract them. These light bulbs emit ultraviolet wavelengths of light that moths are able to detect. A simple lamp against a white sheet can be very effective, while many

A ruddy dagger-wing (Marpesia petreus) alights on a flowery bush to imbibe nectar. Much of the daily life of many butterfly species is taken up with the need to find food and drink.

Newly emerged from their pupae, these bedstraw hawkmoths (Celerio galii) are resting on a tree trunk. The species is a powerful flier; although resident in southern Europe, each year some reach as far north as Britain in their travels.

At rest butterflies hold their wings folded over their bodies so that only the under-wings can be seen. In some species this surface is rather sombre, but the underwings of this Lorquin's admiral (Basilarchia lorquinii) *are extremely attractive.*

Heliconid butterflies, such as this species (Heliconius melpomene), *are widespread in South and Central America. Adults feed on pollen and nectar, and the larvae on leaves of passion vines.*

This pink-spotted sphinx (Agrius cingulatus) is one of the larger and more attractive hawkmoths to be found in North America. Like many of its relatives, it can sometimes be seen feeding on nectar at dusk.

This butterfly (Cethosia biblis) is an attractive species from the Philippines and a member of the family Nymphalidae. Although Asian in origin, the genus is thought by some to be related to the Neotropical heliconid butterflies, since the larvae of both feed on passion vines.

entomologists opt for more sophisticated traps wherein the moths are retained in a box beneath the lamp. The moths are not harmed by the experience and are for the most part extremely docile when examined the following morning. They can then be liberated in the vegetation nearby.

The Future for Butterflies and Moths

Butterflies and moths are arguably the most fascinating of all invertebrate groups and are certainly amongst the most showy and colourful. They have survived the threat of over collecting in the last century but now face new threats. Large-scale, commercial collecting of exotic species as fashionable wall hangings is a growing problem. Greater still is the loss of habitat, which affects butterflies and moths as much as any other group of animals. As free spirits and symbols of the beauty of nature, long may butterflies and moths continue to grace our fields and woodlands in the numbers and varieties that they do today.

INDEX

*Page numbers in **bold-face** type indicate photo captions.*